I0622585

Ed Barrett

PLAY LUCRETIUS

Wet Cement Press
Berkeley, Asheville, Reno

Play Lucretius ©2024 by Ed Barrett
ISBN 979-8-9883840-5-2

Library of Congress Control Number:
2024930156

Cover art:
"Com Dhíneol Surf, Dunquin, Co. Kerry"
by Ciara Barrett

Wet Cement Press
1908 Yolo Ave
Berkeley, CA 94707

www.wetcementpress.com

Acknowledgments

A portion of "Play Lucretius" was included as part of the Boston Renaissance Project of the Woodberry Poetry Room at Harvard University.

A section of "Acis and Galatea" was published in *Cable Street*.

for Jennie

CONTENTS

PLAY LUCRETIUS

1.

a deal with
concrete,
not what it's
made into,
    e.g., the Larz
Anderson Bridge,
curving over the
Charles River
into Allston,
    a discarded
dental floss pick
like a doll's
pirate sword
and a used
condom stuck
to the sidewalk
like a latex emoji

2.

the deal is
it will continue
shot through
with rebar and
belief in laws
unremitting
as Leviticus,
the very ground
beneath my feet
where the Charles
River com-
bined sewer
overflow pipe
unscrolls a
Hokusai heron
stalking its
prey

3.

unremitting lines
of unspeakable
hexameters:
 The New
York Times
reports human
traffickers in
Turkey convicted
of "killing with
eventual intent"
15 Syrian refugees
whose raft
capsized fleeing
to the Greek island
of Kos
 "eventual"
because if
something
turns into
something else
it was
always that

4.

"...25 million
refugees worldwide"
reports *The New
York Times*
     Aeschylus
reports drop by
drop against
our will
some law
of God
drowns the
human heart
unpurged of
images of Alan
Kurdi, age 2,
facedown on the
Turkish shore
     unspeakable
pain that
does not forget

5.

best to place
a mark on the
carriage of cause
and effect
ribboning the
life life
tangles us
up in
      life that
fits so naturally
into its witness
protection program
called nature
      you swear
to be anything
but what you
are and unable
to be
      clarity
awe
      a commonwealth
      ungathered
in shoes of
tar and sand
      a sacred place
beneath my feet
      a criminal
enterprise

6.

seamless voices
constant implacable
decisions and
kidney-shaped
parables
    Show me the
redacted passages
plump with
more tender
words
    "thine"
"a wave
    tossing its
lace panties at
my feet"

7.

    but heaven
holds diplomatic
immunity and
eminent domain
over its children
floating backwards
through the truth
in waves like a
music video
changing expression
and bodies with
biblical disregard
for narrative
    the ocean
chucking their
chins, knocking
off their paper
crowns ringed
with candles like
a birthday cake,
sipping at their
runny noses,
the exchange of
bodily fluids
an ocean
lives for,
hulling out
the body
like a bell

8.

e.g., Mary,
a minor
protected by
rape laws in
the Commonwealth
of Massachusetts,
sole witness to
Gabriel
in painted
Dutch robes
and wings
hovering like
a windmill,
      her mute
Middle Eastern
olive pit eyes
as he crashes
through the door,
one of God's
Navy Seals

9.

　　her arms
outstretched
parting a
pale blue robe,
palms open,
　　her face
turned to the
side in neither
disbelief nor
wonder
　　staring at
pebbles strewn
around her feet
in an Allston
front yard shrine

10.

        her addict
son who basically
abandoned her all
his life missing
an AA meeting
on Antwerp St.,
"a spike in his
arm" as Lenny
calls it, 40
years sober,
retired from the
phone company
with a free
membership to
Blodgett pool
on Soldiers Field
Road, a payoff
from Harvard to
locals when it
was caught
secretly buying
up neighborhood
properties for its
new Allston
campus,
        telling me
when he was
repairing phone lines
he could listen in
on neighborhood
prostitutes talking

and laughing
about their mobster
boyfriends' slobber
in their lap

11.

I'm not especially
religious,
I'm also not
especially un-
religious either,
basically I
swim along
with the
tide
        sometimes
devotion finds
me when I'm
bored shaving,
sometimes
peeing dead center
into the toilet bowl,
my body at its
border, illegal,
trying to cross,
        a burr
on the gown
of being,
        or clomping
around in boots
of character
and fate under
the icy soles
of heaven's sandals—
how they glide

over our dirty
faces turned to
them in their
crystal lacings!

12.

Necessity and
desire
       BBC
nature reruns,
David Atten-
bourough's
benign voice
of fateful, beastful
death,
       Netflix
recommends "for
you, Edward"
Lucretius,
she's a detective,
a real beauty,
living in
an Allston
triple-decker
with her
young son
Chaucer

SHEEPSHEAD BAY, OR THE HEBRIDES

1. Hickory-Q

The second time I went to Coney Island Hospital I stood at the foot of a bed in which a NYPD detective was dying. Coney Island Hospital is not in Coney Island but in Sheepshead Bay, which is now largely Russian, its underworld run by what in Russian slang is called a *Vor*, their word for mafia boss. When I hung out in Sheepshead Bay (not a native, I was a blow-in) it was largely Irish, but its underworld was run by Italian mafia who controlled this lucrative margin lacing up the South Brooklyn shoreline from Gravesend, along the Belt Parkway through Sheepshead Bay (anchored by the Hickory-Q restaurant at the mouth of the bay), around the Jamaica Bay Wildlife Refuge, across Dead Horse Creek to the JFK airport. Their sway didn't cross the Marine Parkway Bridge to Rockaway because white Irish cops and firemen colonized Breezy Point, using an ocean to keep their own kind to itself.

I didn't know what to say to a NYPD detective who was dying. I was a teenager, and he was the father of a kid I didn't really like, but I was there with some friends to pay respect. When his body went into convulsions, the bed rattled, tubes that a moment ago looked like loose mooring lines attached to a boat floating in the bay, jerked around and pulled out. A nurse rushed in, drew a curtain, and I left the room.

A middle-age Irishman looks one of two ways. He's either round-faced and round-bellied; his hair graying or already white, often dyed pitch black but with temples and sideburns left white to show (I think) the carriage of age is dignified, ripening with wisdom, but it always reminded me of an unfinished aluminum siding job on a two-story house. Or he's tall and lean, with a full head of wavy brown hair. The NYPD detective in his hospital bed was that kind: TV cop-show good looks, handsome face with Samuel Beckett cheek angles, sharp as anchor flukes digging into silt at the bottom of Sheepshead Bay to hold a mooring in place.

There's a certain kind of grace in not always killing everyone with good looks, which he must have found hard to appreciate. It's not good policy, fatal charm. Best to keep such an unearned gift out of the spotlight. Since he lived in Sheepshead Bay and his precinct was in South Brooklyn, he'd stop by the boat club. Other men with normal jobs were at work while their wives and children enjoyed summer vacation. He cut a figure in his detective suit and would casually put a hand in his trouser pocket to flash a small brown holster at his side. Wives and mothers playing cards around umbrellaed tables took note, but in a way that also showed they recognized his arrogance, maybe in self-defense against their own straying thoughts (*Does he think he can pick me up like that!*) drifting in the salty air.

Funny what you know but don't know in the nearness of things to come, an eventual intent that fits so perfectly into its witness protection program called life, not guilty of a crime, more like a criminal enterprise, twisty as an octopus on BBC Planet Earth, its head like a wrinkly scrotum squeezing into places you'd never think of to kill in the natural way of things we accept, one scene after another, seamless as an NFL replay of what we just saw, a last act recognition we now learn we should have seen coming; then a whispered swoosh sound to show we're back in the present, where bored eyes linger along a summer's blue and white day as poised and graceful hulls shift softly around their moorings with the tide.

He looked good enough in his detective suit and holster to make his point. But on this, his day off, in civilian clothes—plaid shirt, belted khaki pants, no holstered gun—he didn't draw out an idle midday mother's thoughts, women sunning themselves who had already taken his measure. They saw what was in it for them with him, good Irish Catholic grammar school graduates who knew how to diagram life as a series of sentences with prepositional phrases.

He was just there, idle and encumbered by having nothing to do while mothers were busy watching their children playing near the water. So, when two Italian teenage kids, outsiders, playing on the beach below the women's card tables started cursing really loud, he took it as a chance to draw some female gazes his way by assuming these women were offended by rude language. He climbed down the bulkhead to the beach, told the kids to shut up, and when one of them said fuck you, his policeman bravado kicked in and he slapped the kid around. The kids ran off, he climbed back up, all eyes on him.

A little later two men showed up. They were thick as wood oarlocks on the gunwale of a row boat used for work around piers as it rocks against pilings encrusted with mussels in their shiny black Caravaggio helmets which its hull scrapes off in clusters or smashes open, their dull orange tongues twisted out. I can't figure out why he didn't recognize the kids he slapped around belonged to the minor mafia godlings who owned the Hickory-Q restaurant at the mouth of the bay. He was a cop and should know these things. Maybe he did see them for who they were in that slivering moment when eyes that were fogged unfog, but felt he had to finish what he started or suffer the scorn of mothers watching. To be honest, I'm more astonished that the oarlocks sent to beat him up knew, but didn't care, that he was a cop. All this changed how I think about sway and balance and decisions.

2. Sheepshead Bay, or the Hebrides

The first time I went to Coney Island Hospital was after I won a game of handball.

One-wall handball was invented by James VI of Scotland, later James I of England and Ireland, he of the englished Bible, the Sheldon Adelson of his age for financing Bible translators, the King James Bible "*whose mortal taste*" of divinity one could argue "*Brought Death into the world... With loss of Eden.*" One-wall handball translated easily into Brooklyn, brought in by Irish and Scottish immigrants; a street sport for marginalized areas, those Scotlands to their Englands, those outlaw clans with their outlawed tongues.

The outdoor handball court where I played in Sheepshead Bay was regulation size. The wall was made of wood, like most early 20th century beach handball courts; the floor was poured concrete, scored with one thin contraction joint going side to side, which we used as the service line. Court sidelines weren't marked, but where the concrete floor met parking-lot asphalt was the right court side boundary; on the left side there was a narrow lane of dirt and gravel on which a massive weathered wood beam marked the sideline. In winter, the court was a dry dock for smaller boats taken out of their slips along the pier. Each spring they were returned to the bay, and the court was swept clean of dried-out seaweed and other debris scraped off their hulls from the tides they carried on.

I learned to play handball against the wall of Key Food Supermarket. The curb was the service line, and sidelines were marked by cars parked on either end of the No Standing Loading Zone which gave us a space wide enough to play. My cousin Billy taught me how to play handball. He came to live with my family a year before I was born (my mother was told she couldn't have children). He had been abandoned at age seven by his mother. My mother's other sister, who lived in Saugus MA, took him for a couple of years, but her new boyfriend didn't want him hanging around, so he was sent back to Brooklyn. My mother had already taken in her father, who was an immigrant from Scotland by way of England, and my father's sister who, after her husband was murdered over a gambling debt, was living with a man in Coney Island until he dumped her and she had nowhere else to go and just showed up at the door of the one-bedroom apartment where my parents lived. Housing six people in a one-bedroom tenement apartment is more challenging than the geometry of hitting an ace in a handball court. The floor beneath my feet was their sanctuary, confused of grace.

My mother wasn't especially religious. Born Protestant, she left an abusive home when she was a teenager; she converted to Catholicism because she was pretty and went to dances in Catholic dance halls in South Brooklyn, and the boys liked her, but the Catholic schoolgirls would beat her up because they were jealous and she was an outsider. A bit of chrism on the forehead and problem solved. The only Catholic thing she believed in was Mary because I think she identified with her, a young girl who lived what I think anyone would agree was a tough life.

Ancestry.com story lines are really just stage directions which leave you in a borrowed spotlight, center stage with bellows for a prop, bellows big as a whale, big enough to choke a whale burrowing its wormholes through the migrant ocean's devastated memory. The theater itself is a prop, a bellows balanced on the narrow mouth of its cone-shaped voice; an axle through your neck and your breast and your thigh.

I'm amphibious about religion, but sometimes I pray to Mary because my mother said when she prayed to her, it helped. I'm surprised to find myself praying silently when I'm running steps in the Harvard stadium in Allston, my lips closed, my tongue moving in braille inside my mouth.

3. Killer

I'm not sure what to think about a soul inhabiting me distinct from my body which ribbons it. Or where it goes when that ribbon is untied. I feel like something's "there," like we all do, something singular, compact as the period at the end of this sentence.

"25 million refugees worldwide, reports the NYT." I copied that down in a notebook smeared with blobs of ink-gel from a PILOT G-2 pen. And what followed it? A list of things I left behind in Ireland, followed by a page of numbers calculating car rentals for two months. That was followed by a page with a note to myself about the time I went to the Two Brothers barber shop at 7pm, long after the time when children got haircuts (I was six) and heard one of the twin barber-brothers ask, basically to the whole shop which seemed to be following his monologue, "All she's got is a big twat, and whaddaya gonna do with that?" I knew about the basic parts of sex and some of its procedures, and I figured this question was a slur against a neighborhood woman (probably all women). It stuck with me enough that the next day I asked my best friend Jimmy what he thought about this. Jimmy was as good-natured as a loaf of fresh baked bread, never a crude word or thought. Without hesitating he replied, "Twat did you say, I cunt hear you, I am hard-on hearing." He seemed surprised and pleased at his cunning witticism, and turned and walked away like Oscar Wilde in a cape with a walking stick made out of Sylvania 60-watt light bulbs all lit up.

So naturally everything fits into the background, receding just at the point where you try to enter it.

If you believe you have a soul, it's probably some combination of desire, expectation, necessity, fate (or character: character is fate, clomping around in goofy cothurni). Sort of like your kitchen drawer that holds unused screws of different sorts and sizes, stamps, unsorted rubber bands, small hooks to hang something with; things you'll need for later on, so much stuff that I can never find the one thing I'm looking for, and I know it's in there, that which I feel the absence of.

So, basically, we inhabit an eventual intent all the time where the stage directions read *Exeunt omnes* and *Enter, you*, as I ran across the handball court hitting the ball with the palm of my hand, an action repeated by the Italian kid I was playing against, both of us making a *slap slap slap* sound like waves applauding up the side of a lapstrake hull, his cross-court shot bouncing fair and about to go out of bounds marked by the wood-beam boundary line before I could return it; and it felt like one of those "spots in time" Wordsworth—of all people!—described before he went gaga with his clump of Ecclesiastical Sonnets, dull and bulky as the Galway Cathedral or a Super Bowl ring; moments, he wrote, "that with distinct pre-eminence retain/A renovating virtue, whence...our minds/ Are nourished and invisibly repaired," like I was gliding along a frozen Dutch canal in those ice skates with long blades you see in Flemish oil paintings, instead of sneakers across concrete, my left arm swinging up, then down and along the surface of the wood beam as I returned the shot before it went out of bounds, a thick piece of that weathered wood beam stabbing under my fingernail into the faint half-moon at the bottom of the nail, deep enough that I had to go to the emergency room at Coney Island Hospital to have it cut out. But I had hit an ace, the ball shooting fair straight back from the bottom of the wall without a sliver of Lucretian space between it and the ground, a killer, a real killer.

Naked as a Dime (a Pastoral)

1. Acis and Galatea

daylight
feeds the sky
its measure
of blood,
all hearts
felt ready

a sign marked
"Lime Kilns,"
credulous Acis,
all desire
and mud,
suing fluvial
love, Galatea's
immortal voltage

and miraculously
the sun installed
its clips without
snapping them,
nets of figures
moved with
air draped
near the water
that trusts
in reaching
something
separated,
stalks of
Galatea algae
rooted in silt
and desire and
pursuit

glorious loving
avarice
is a beautiful
nullification,
no essence
suppressing
the body
of its armor,
blood and love,
a mythology
with its own
tolling,
lunging and
diffusing its
iconic predicaments
in a vivacious scene

who then
if stepping
from a scene
swerves
in the alcove
where the stream
is so cold it
makes you dizzy?
who then
says "crystal
net, you
constellations,
you fall
all over me,
my face gives
you contour,
gives you
my cheek bones,
my breath,
sweet as
a cherry
sleigh bed,
a human
problem, the
letter I
hungry for
reasons,
the letter
I, spinning
there on itself?"

Galatea "is
not entirely
convinced
the move to
take back
the body
will last"
("Behold the
New Naked,"
in *Thursday
Styles, The
New York Times*
10/20/22)
It's the fashion
to be immersed,
turned by
one hand as
in the other
a slow sharp
blade tries
to achieve
that perfect
citrus spiral,
an orange
rind unraveling
over the
countertop

yes, as you
wrote: "each
fossil immortal
act," plaited
with mud,
plaited with
songs, immortal
of wishes,
immortal of
lies, divine thises
and thatses,
muddy lungs,
plaited with ribs,
falling head
over heels
in love, the
currency of life
changing dark
seaweed dollar
green into
blouse and
summer skirt
pastels of lighter
euro notes

as if you
held a shell
over your
eyes and
saw the ocean
toss its pearl
slip and white
foam panties
at your feet
and you think
you can reach
through the shower
curtain of your
body into these
immortal waves
like a child
reaching for
a shiny shell

life's borders
gerrymandered
into shapes
exotic as insects
on BBC Planet
Earth, real
life, but,
who'd've
imagined such
creatures
in the ground
beneath your
feet, or
trapezing,
aerial, weightless,
nimble in
devastation and
wonder
in the air
we breathe

insidious,
immortal
voltage grabs
our daily
iconographic
predicaments in
secret alcoves
because divine
Galatea
loves freshness
and the buckets
of paint that
will narrate
her stepping
into a scene
countrified at
the core, her
eye trained
on a body,
its glorious
loving avarice
grabbing at
freshness

and as a
leaf buds on
Ancestry.com,
login name
"Ovid,"
oh hopeful
Ovid, so
downstream,
such verdurelicious
lingering

2. All Souls' Night

all the bells
in Ovid are
never heard
over the ocean's
tolling monastery
bells, "that gong
tormented sea,"
as Yeats called it,
his fluency
with ghosts,
wound up
in that world,
"As mummies in
the mummy-cloth
are wound...."
It's an Irish
thing. I'm Irish,
raised Catholic,
now out of grace.
I still say
"Holy Ghost"
instead of
Holy Spirit.
And tonight is
All Souls'
Night when
our lips part
and speak to,
or through,
what separates
lingerers-on

down here
from the fleet
deer-hooved
dead up there,
immortally,
whether they
like it or not,
and I'm in line
for coffee
at the coffee
shop whose
cold-brew
coffee apparatus
is straight out of
Frankenstein which
has flooded TV
all this week before
Halloween along
with *The Mummy*.
Young Boris
Karloff was very
handsome. At a
dinner party
we went
around the table
saying (invoking?)
what actor and actress
we thought was
most beautiful.
I said young Boris
Karloff and young
Barbara Stanwyck,
their images from

movies, "moving
pictures," as what
we now hallow
as "film" once
were called, my
daughter's diploma
in film from
Trinity College
Dublin, her
diploma written
in Latin: *Studia
de Simulacris
Moventibus*,
"Studies in
Moving Pictures,"
Latin so suave,
promoting
its eternity
over our
branch of days.
I laughed out
loud reading
Yeats's "Adam's
Curse" when
the line "I strove/
to love you
in the old high
way of love"
was misprinted as
"I strove/
to love you
in the old
highway of love...."

—the old highway of love

and what "old
way" was Yeats
thinking of, all
those story lines
tangled up like
linguini in myths
and operas,
couplings and
killings, fate
and its narrative
slowly rolling over
like a capsized
oil tanker as
a chorus of
wetland sedges
and seabirds
exit stage right

3. CVS

a robot
voice says
"I'll put you
on hold for
a brief time,
please stay
on the line."
Held and
holding.
Blub blub
if I let go
and drown
in the rush
of high
call volumes,
a choice,
a Lucretian
sliver of choice
in which my
memory holds
for me a late
afternoon on
the west coast
of Ireland, rough
surf and a wave,
backlit by a
setting sun,
held still
by a stiff offshore
wind, the wave's
serrated knife-

edge curl I
thought was
a line of birds
taking flight
not to scale,
like life,
the sketchy
design where
things will go,
its own reasons
for this particular
scatter of givens
that inhabit
invisible lines,
parallels, the
countrified
dimensions of
thought and
desire. "There's
no such thing
as the next best
thing to love," James
Darren sings to
Sandra Dee in
the surfing movie
Gidget, and he
surfs down
the curling
song wave
mysteriously
as he smoothly
punches above
his weight with

the next line,
"Necessity gave
the cold, cold
hand a glove."
Where did that
come from and
what did it mean?
CVS puts me
on hold. My
prescriptions
put me on hold,
delaying through
my bloodstream
me being transferred
to that furthest,
dread end
of nature,
or if I choose to
"hear this menu again,"
my iPhone screen
smeared against
my ear, I'll have
to listen to looping
out-of-this-world
music, and who
at CVS thought
this theme was
soothing while
you're hanging on,
floating backward
through the truth?

4. Naked as a Dime

two women
walking ahead of
me on Brattle
Street discussing
their friend's
wedding gown,
and one says,
"She looked
naked as a dime."
And when I
thought about
it, I could see
how that could
describe a
silvery, tight
dress, what
fluvial Galatea
looked like to
dusty Acis,
more than
either of them
could change
and didn't
want to
because desire
is myopic as
a flea circus
with invisible
performances
on invisible wires,
invisible, vivacious

scenes trained
on the definite
in love
with freshness
and if to
step out of
this scene,
the body of
the definite,
its nakedness
a monologue,
smears riverbed
mud and algae
all over your
sunny ankles
tangled in
rushes that
swerve through
your hair
loving freshness
in the direction
of Galatea

About the Author

Ed Barrett is the author of ten books of poetry, most recently *The Leaves Are Something This Year, New and Selected Prose Poems* (2023). He was born in Brooklyn NY and pursued an MFA at Brooklyn College and received a PhD from Harvard where he studied English literature, Greek and Irish. His family home is in Dunquin, Co. Kerry, Ireland. He resides in Cambridge MA where he is Senior Lecturer in Creative Writing at MIT.